THE WEATHER GODS

Sarah Etlinger

Fernwood
PRESS

The Weather Gods

©2022 by Sarah Etlinger

Fernwood Press
Newberg, Oregon
www.fernwoodpress.com

Printed in the United States of America

Cover and page design: Mareesa Fawver Moss

Author photo: Abbye Portzen

Cover photo: Elizabeth Lies via Unsplash

ISBN 978-1-59498-093-0

ACKNOWLEDGMENTS

"We Do Not Yet Know All the Ways" *Royal Rose*, May 2019.

"Late Summer," "Peaches," "Eurydice Summons Orpheus Back to the Underworld for One Night," "Wren," "Full," "Antidote" (as "Disguise"), and "Evanescence with Clouds" (as "Equinox") *Eunoia*, February 2020.

"If I Told You I Loved You, It Would Be the Wrong Thing to Say" *Bramble*, July 2019.

"Transfer" *The Pangolin Review*, January 2020.

"Into Knowing," "That Day We Walked the Beach" (as "Better Than We Could Dream to Be—"), and "Something like Light" *Amethyst Review*, October 2019.

"Time Equals Distance over Speed," "Bric-a-Brac," "Love Poem with Pansies (as "All We Are") *Crepe & Penn* 4, October 2019.

"Currency" and "As the Crow Flies (as "Watershed") *Vita Brevis*, April 2020.

"The Naming" *Mookychick*, August 2019.

"City of Robins" *Spry*, Summer 2020.

"Rehearsal" *Poetica*, Summer 2020.

"Pillow Talk 1" *Royal Rose*, Summer 2019.

"Pillow Talk 2" and "Zeus Contemplates His Encounter with Leda While Awaiting His Rape Trial" *Never One for Promises,* 2018.

"Leda's Dream" *The Cabinet of Heed*, February 2020.

"Mating Season" Vessel 2 (Now defunct).

"I Worried All Night about the Birds" *Ghost City Review*, September 2019.

AUTHOR'S NOTES

Many writers often feel isolated from others, even when they move through the world daily. Yet after more than a year of isolation in which all aspects of everyone's lives were disrupted, it feels somehow miraculous to be writing this note of appreciation. Despite the perceived and real isolation, so many people have offered their support—so many people and so many small blessings that, once again, I find myself lacking the words to express my gratitude. I am so very grateful for this book to finally come into the world, warts and all. The following people have supported me in the same way—with grace, compassion, and unwavering acceptance; as always, without them, this book would not be here.

First, thank you to my exceptional editor, Eric Muhr, and the staff at Fernwood Press. Your work is a true mitzvah: you make beautiful things, and the world is better for it. Thank you for your patience, your kindness, and your expertise on this book.

I would also like to offer thanks to my reviewers: DeMisty Bellinger, Lannie Stabile, and Derrick Harriell. You saw so much in this book that I didn't, and I am so grateful for your careful attention in this busy and frustrating time.

Heartfelt thanks and gratitude once again to Kathleen Dale, whose expertise and honesty makes everything better. I thank you for seeing this book's potential, even when I didn't, and for understanding where this book wanted to go.

Few poets are as lucky as I am to have Dr. Elizabeth Johnston Ambrose as a reader. Your painstaking attention to every single word and your unflagging patience is unmatched. I cannot thank you enough for all the writing we do together and the ways you help my work develop. Thank you for writing with me and for your inspiration.

To my friends and colleagues who never stop showing up to offer support, answer my ridiculous questions, and encourage me to do this: you do not realize how much all you do helps me to stay inspired. In particular, Gabby Bachhuber, Kelly Baran, Valerie Blair, Allison Castillo, Becky and Dan Hansen, Tracy Kruse, Liana Odrcic, Martin Quirk, Alexis Whyte, Lisa Woodall, and Kevin Wozniak, make all of this possible. Thank you all for being you.

No less important is the support I receive daily from my husband, Brad Houston. Thank you for always being my #1 fan, even if you don't get it or understand what it is I do. Your love has always made my life possible and more enriching. And to my son, Gabriel, whose questions, curiosity, and love for language never cease to amaze me. I'm so glad I get to share this world with you.

And to the rest of my family—my parents, sister, and extended relatives—your support for all of my writing endeavors has been a beacon in the storm. If not for your encouragement and commitment to my success, I would not have done any of this. Every day I am more and more grateful for what you have given me throughout my life.

Finally, to Molly Sides, a friend who feels like family and shows us the way in all things, I offer my deepest appreciation. This book is for you.

TABLE OF CONTENTS

I.

TRANSFER

I don't believe in ghosts or God,
even though you do
(and sometimes I wish I could).
You carry them in your pocket
along with your flashlight and wallet.

I want to open the door
to the sky and let the gods amble in.
I'd sit them down, offer them coffee,
a piece of pound cake.
We might have a nice afternoon
in spite of me.

You say if I am just quiet enough,
they'll come in by themselves,
fill the gaps between things.
That's what faith is, after all, you say—for the gaps.

I'm not so sure: the gaps are where I love you,
the little ruts in time where
desire wriggles in, hopeful
as dawn's first gasp over the earth.

At night, in sleep, you find a peaceful god
wrapped up in a bead.
I take it from you, hold it to my chest,
wish for transfer.

A train passes outside the window
in the dark. The moon slips behind a cloud.

WE DO NOT YET KNOW ALL THE WAYS

our hearts can break:

how could we know
all the cracks and fault lines,
when the bends and curves
of terrain have not been crossed;

how could we know
what we'll require
when we are left, pitched
in leaky tents and shivering
with nothing but wet leaves for beds?

We cannot know these things
without maps, without valleys and rivers
carved into our skins
from love's worn compass;

we do not know yet
how we will crave
the scents of love
spent tapering the night
down to melted wax,
or how your hands
learn mine the way dew
learns the curve
of grass blades;

we have not yet come to know
just how, when morning sighs
and the sun insists
it's time for warmth,
we are already waiting
like water on sleep's surface,
with ink
on our fingertips
to draw the map,
fill in the broken lines,
show us where
the path will fork.

If I Told You I Loved You,
It Would Be the Wrong Thing to Say

You come in from slaughtering the chickens,
your hand still spattered
with blood, and your eyes
have that quiet I've come to accept
on days like today

where we're aware of the order of things,
of the fact that the same hands
that hold the chickens' necks,
slowly swinging them above your head
before carrying them, upside down,
into the killing cone
for the final cut,

are the same hands
that coax me to love, the same
tender fingers I've come to expect
just as much as the sunrise in the morning,
its blush on the day
rosy as your skin after a shower
before you slide into bed with me.

You stand in the doorway, now,
a white towel in your hands.
You smile at me with your quiet smile
(the one I've come to expect, to want)
as you take your place on the pillow,
and, arms akimbo behind your head,
your eyes blink, close, sleep.

ANTECEDENT

It was the old truck that did it.
Same year, same color, but without the lumpy belt of rust
lining the grate, and without the missing gas cap.
Otherwise, identical.

I'd been walking in the neighborhood,
admiring the pool of pansies humming in the wind.
I could watch you walk with the wind in your hair like that forever,
you'd said.

You might've, if winter hadn't come, if we'd stayed.
I never told you how, looking at the sun,
I wished for you.
Every time day cracked into windows,
I felt your face there.

The first time I felt it, we drove in your truck
and used pliers for the heater knobs.

Before: a mellow gray, cold, unstuck
by our laughter.
After: the thump of a heartbeat washed with light,
like love that is not in the world yet.
Now: spring as a raindrop on the windowpane,
an ache in the grass.

LOVE POEM IN THREE ACTS

i.

Last year we sat in grubby lawn chairs among the burgeoning blooms.
This year, the chairs are stacked in the garage
since spring blew in early—
reminding us of last year's snow.
What I really mean is each time spring comes we forget a little of what
it looked like last year, except we still search for the violets
in the grass, the snowdrops with their wet fairy heads,
the burning daffodils, the heavy hyacinths,
the whispers of pussy willows, the brief hour of forsythia.
By the time the lilacs burst out screaming on the branches,
we've accepted it. We forget what we once knew:
we see so little.

Actually, it's a lot like this:
we tell love by the knots in the heart.
This, the story of the house and the family.
This imagines the garden.
This is the birthday cake from your late mother's recipe.
This is the dreamed-of picnic out on the beach by the lake,
my hair uncurling in the wind, your hands on my bare feet,
wine and fruit staining our throats.
This—the thickest—is the photo of me unaware,
green shirt against Christmas lights.

Love is just a longing for things to be different,
a dirge made in your throat as it calls
today is today is today is

ii.

What do we know of walls
until they surround us
with their sturdy everydayness,
all cement and poles,
like cities struck up against lightning,
invisible until we are inside them?

In this light
my body is a wall of glass,
a translucent fortress,
an ancient city,
a burial ceremony
with hollow eulogy
tilling the earth
like winter over water,
rain over sand,
stones over skin.

A bell sounds at the bottom of a lake,
its echo in puddles.
My voice feels like a bird
in high wind stretched full.

Shards of our existence crumble
into seasons, slivers of ragged glass
and sand in my toes at the lake
at the beach.
On the very best day,
we still see so little,
tell so little of what we are.

iii.

Remember the story of the little white house
with the little family and the little dog
and the dog sometimes runs away and the wife says
she's going to kill her husband for leaving the gate open
but then the dog always comes back
so you say *forgive your husband*
there's so much of myself in him
he's a good husband
you're a good wife and there's no good
on the other side
and he loves you in all the right ways
and so do you oh yes so do you

Love is just a longing
lingering in the lengthening summer light
where the trees yearn in the wind
oh yes so do you so do you

When Spring Turns to Summer

We are not bound to bodies—
we only write on them
with ink forged from time
and water,

    and when it all washes away
    in the heavy
    spring raindrops
    that drench the soul,

all that's left
is summer's perennial stain,
golden light
pulsing in the grass.

BACKYARD IN AUGUST

This heavy season full of everything glistening,
      golden black-eyed Susans drowned in light,
tousled in a clump of weeds,
      ivy twisting its shoulders along lattice fences
propped against houses and porches;

      from where I sit on the patio, the prim
solemn rows of identical chimneys crowning roofs along
      the block, one after the other after the other,
strung along the power lines and wires, spines
      arching and flexing to support our precarious lives,

against the brocade of trees,
      leaves still richly green, a quivering bas-relief
for the splotches of birds and birdsong
      in the stew of swirling clouds,
in the vast blue later hung with star-drift
      and deep darkening pierced only by fireflies—

all of it on display, summer in Technicolor poured in
      to every crack and space, everywhere everything
breathing and moving and deepening,
      all of it, all of it
together, nothing seems lonely.

THE STORY

I keep thinking of the story you told me
about that woman in college who opened her robe to you
when you came to pick up your cake
and the fact that you left without realizing what she intended—
by then it was too late, outside by the car,
holding the cake, kicking pebbles with your feet—
without realizing that maybe she loved you, too,
as much as you loved her.

I'm thinking about it now because I like its irony,
and I'm always looking for irony in everyday places,
like a sign that says "Vacancy" at an abandoned motel.
But more than that, I like it because it shows
how naïve we really are. How, in the end,
the stars didn't align, how she might have better understood
that the night she chose to bare her body to you
(the only thing one ever really owns)
was not the night you needed it.
No, you needed it differently, in summer
when evenings lengthen into night, slow as tide.

You wouldn't have known that, then:
not even the night you told me the story; I didn't think
either of us knew what we needed. I was still perched on the fainting couch
in your hotel room, the crisp ink-dark of November night
for backdrop, you sprawled on your bed, barefoot.
I remember thinking I'd never seen your bare feet,
how you kept looking at the ceiling while you were talking.
I remember telling you the story was sad but that it was like you,

and then, when you said,
I haven't even told you the end of it yet:
the worst part is, she left school the following week,
and then, that summer, my neighbor's son told me
he had to spend three full hours in the car
with her best friend hearing how I had ruined her life.
—Then it wasn't you, I said, *she didn't communicate,*
she should have told you—and that's the irony:

neither of you could have ever said the thing to be said,
that the universe keeps playing chicken with the truth.
Even if we could have said, could ever say or know
the one thing we need,
it is never enough, always uneven,
the way dreams often do come true, large and loud
like the rush of wind on the prairie.

It's there, in a sudden gasp that bends the grass
into Möbius, then disappears—
leaving only the memory or the traces,
a few broken stalks, scattered seeds.

Ex Nihilo

We say nothing comes from nothing—
only God creates something out of nothing.

Metaphor—what we'll say when we want something
to be what it isn't, to stretch to meet our expectations.

A field of corn to say *I love you.*

A knock-kneed stance to say *I need saving.*

A god to say *I'd like to keep on living—*

The silent, quiet *o* in our throats
as we call out to each other. *I'm sorry. I'm sorry.*

What we've called *corn* we rip from stalks,
smell the sweet earth at bronzed necks.

We'll say we've reaped what we've sown—
all those sun-hours hunched earthward.

And we'll say we believe in God, in a whole world
beyond. Isn't that why we're here

with a whole mess of vegetables waiting in the cellar?
Nothing until something, and then another thing entirely.

Time Equals Distance over Speed

The thing is, there are many ways to measure time:
seasons, years, eons, hours, sunlight;

there's the way time passes when we're driving,
scenes pausing for less than seconds
before rearranging themselves back into blur;

there's the way light curtsies on summer leaves
in a flamenco with the sky;

the spaces between breaths,
brief when you're with me,
long as your sleep;

there are egg timers and sand timers
and many many millions of parsecs,

ways to measure spaces between words,
syllables, phonemes,

ways to measure distance (87 miles, exactly)
to get to you, or 1 hour and 22 minutes
(less if the wind is right and no traffic),

the way wind slows us down
or lengthens, lets us fly like quicksilver
along the invisible angles
we call the earth,

the hour the clouds become angels
shifting and remaking all the things we'll ever see
and how long it takes to notice one thing
or the other before it all disappears into nothing,

yet nothing measures the lengths
I've gone to forget
the things I should not want.

INTO KNOWING

Let me imagine you
into knowing
as a shadow,
a glass,
a heavy whisper
trying to span the space
between what we can be
and our sins—

—our sins only that we think to pray at all,
asking with compass hearts
for time, time—bundled hours
where we can mend holes,
the stain of ethics,
the weight of truth and light.

Let me imagine you
as a long pause,
brief clutches
of breath and cadence
in the sentence we could
would become, if only loss
were not so dear,
if love were ever just.

BLUEBERRIES

I wanted to ask you why you were already gone,
but you were already gone.

Sometimes I still crave your shape
to tuck into my mouth for safekeeping.

A bowl of blueberries waits on the counter
for pie, an offering.

AS THE CROW FLIES

Where are you now if not here?
Don't tell me why—just come to me
as a crow flies through a hole in the air,
oil-slicked and glistening, with a ragged stone
in its beak.

I whistle into newly-swollen streams,
stand where knees of boats have touched the shore,
pray to be held by the wallop of water.

The dark is no place for hiding:
my heart creaks under the weight of it all.

Above me, planes clutch light,
don't let go, tether their orbits.

If I bend or fall, a crow will gather
the pieces I was, tuck them away,
fly back into a braid of air.

Pillow Talk (1)

I said
I can't remember a time
when I wasn't anxious
it is like the ocean,
its giant loom
clacking with the warp
and weft of the waves,
loud and rushing,
weaving jagged kisses
on the surface
and jittery rolls
into the sand,
water always ankle-deep
and hissing.

He said
I just worry about you.
I try to smile
to reassure him
I am fine, the ocean
lives around me
inside my mind too,
and I am used to it;
after all, I grew up
going to the beach,
my toes rooting in the sand,
its mottled streaks
dribbling down my arms
to make dripcastles

and the constant call
of seagulls waiting for morsels,
onyx tangles of seaweed
littering the beach,
salt down to my bones
that ached from swimming,
from battling the tide.

He said
I love you
and I kiss him,
finally pulling him in.

Eurydice Summons Orpheus Back to the Underworld for One Night

Tonight I have chosen you
(my once and future love)—
you are wary, as if the weight
of time has pressed your skin
into coal, obsidian fossils,
not the ruddy bronze
that had loved me into song.

But you take my hand as if destined
(as I have already forgiven),
and we dart like minnows
in between raindrops;
our skin tastes their salt,
their sediment, the gravity
reminding us of our bodies, forms
immortal and not.

We only get one love:
just as there is only one story
and one song you ever sang,
there is only one love—
we just keep loving the same
again and again;
perhaps through time
or bodies, one love starts
our heartbeats, pulls us
earthward, toward forks—

left, here,
right, there;
this love points like this;
that one looks like that,
and straight ahead is nowhere
we could ever be.

I stand with you behind me
at the precipice of a question,
its voice a ripple through the clouds—
tonight we forgive,
tomorrow we go back.

ANTIDOTE

We are never at the mercy of anything
but grief's pull—thick worn ropes aching
and straining under waves to eke the boats in
against the tide.

Maybe it's the physics of it all
that haunts us, astonishes us, dwarfs us—
particles ever humming and swirling;

maybe it's the magnitude of it all,
the tilt of the orbits and poles,
the equinox, the seasons, the wind
arcing across cattails.

Mercy does not come as easily as the tide,
as light through the window looking around
for something before disappearing.

Maybe it is love's touch on the back of the day,
careful as the moon brooding sluggish in the heavens
as it carves paths the meadows track across hills,
the mounds of corn slowly crawling to reach the milk-washed
winter sky, edging ever closer, away from loss.

THE NAMING

Still cloaked in winter pants, we sat
in the backyard to admire the chickens.

We found your son's sock he'd thrown off
as he squished in the new mud;
we chased him around the yard, so he wouldn't go into the street
where the neighbors were all out like the new buds—
washing cars, picking up branches, cleaning windows.
We laughed when he brought us half a flower he'd plucked
and crushed. You put it in my hand as if
it were the natural order of things.

Then you showed me the garden,
still craggy and weary from winter.
Here are the branches of forsythia.
Here is the tree we bought last year on Mother's Day
(a cherry).
Here are the crocus beds. The daffodils.
I could see their twisted stems already,
and *here's where I'd like to put hydrangeas.*

How about violets? I asked.
My mother grew African violets.
There's an embroidered picture, I said, *that came with my house.*
Yes, it's a sign, you said, and then we watched the boys across the street.

When I left, you didn't turn to look at me,
didn't wave or smile, even though I waited.
I only saw the open garage door, then the mailbox,
then you gathering your mail, your now-bare feet
hobbling along the gravel. You'd bring it in,
set it on the table, make neat piles.
I saw the evening light bending
in my rearview mirror,
as if to wedge a space between us.

Then, ducks and crows called above us,
as if pointing and naming the growing things,
the things with potential, the things that could be.

I'VE MISTAKEN

early April rain
for spring

this sudden closeness
for love.

PEACHES

She can no longer taste the peaches of her childhood.

No one sells them in the markets,
and they've hybridized the variety.
But traces linger in her memory,
nestle like baby birds
against the roof of her mouth.

No name exists for the smell of grass
except *the smell of grass*—
exactly what it is,
sweet, sharp scent signaling summer.
There's even a name for the sound of s-es:
sibilants, and *petrichor* names
the scent of rain on the dry soil,
often the first scent of the season.

You told me
you only have love
as a sense-memory:
the curl of hair on a neck
or the smell of a woman—
how she seems so holy
so serene and almost numb
to that kind of good sleep
that comes when, having shared
planes and heartbeats, one must
fall back into time again.

The body and heart
remember what words do not.
The world will go on,
and our cells reach for each other
only because they must.
Somewhere there's an invisible light
calling them toward erosion,
toward home.

WREN

we huddle under blankets
to see how close our knees can get

we watch the snow
sift down from the heavens

listening to its eulogy
for fall, the cracking bare trees

knowing the whole time
that spring will come,

then summer
for us to dream of,

dreams we carry
in our hands and breath,

right as the winter morning
flies in on bird wings,

one lone
wren

FULL

I can fill a cup of tea, watch it breathe as it settles.
I can kiss a winter afternoon full of blue light.
I can fill a cup with yes, with you, with one flawless winter hour—

outside, ice glazes windows and water
so clear we believe we can see through it,
full of fish, all the way to the bottom.

Enough of It

In my cloak of wickedness I dream you're dead,
hidden under the cracked stage of ice
on the lake where only I can see you.
Even fish don't bother you. They swim up and peck,
see your wrinkles and pallor and how deep
your eyes have grown.
Only fringes of algae embrace you, snarling on your limbs.
I twist a thread of it, haul you to the surface,
warm myself to your bones.
When I breathe again, I am blue fire,
and you ignite my lungs with the flint
you've saved for occasions such as this
—and then you are nothing but
curls of ash smoldering on the ice.

Awake, now, I think I am too wicked:
no one would store the tools of their own immolation
this way. You told me once you wanted to die in your sleep.
Something instant. Irreversible. A giant crash of thunder
or a sudden gasp of wind under which you'd vanish.
But I don't believe you would actually go this way.

Instead, it would be piecemeal, something like sainthood:
an arm amputated by a tractor accident,
a hunk of kneecap shaved off. Shoulder clipped.
A runt piglet that you nursed hourly for days
tucked to your chest, the exhaustion of incessant care
the flood that finally drowned you.
You'll look up at the rains coming on,
the smear of sky grayer and grayer as it descends
with the slow determination of floodwater,

wind pricking up its ears. Beyond the farmhouse,
the fields will lean back, point toward horizon,
right themselves. And then there's my face in the watery mud,
clinging to the boots you still wear out of habit.

Maybe I am wrong. Maybe I never knew you at all.
Maybe it really is too wicked to imagine how you would die,
though sometimes I relish the taste of it
as it plays on my tongue like the sweet milky musk
of those fresh apples you used to hand me
so gently, from the cellar, where we sat on crates
chewing the fruits of your labor
before coming back upstairs
to miss the things we wished we were.

Maybe spring is indeed as good as love gets:
everything rushes toward blooming, to metaphor.
What if we were daffodils or regal magnolias
with their throbbing pink buds bursting from the branches
just to show off, just for the sake of it?
What would we do if we dawned, like morning, only for possibility?
If our hearts caught butterflies in nets we never let go?
If the black river ran faster?
If the rain held only our faces, could we kiss and float,
kites far above the blue?
Maybe we could fly.

Enough of this feathered dreaming.
Today I let a feather go,
thinking of how it would surf and coast on the wind,
land somewhere rattled by its journey.
Someone else will find it, admire the good fortune
of such a perfect spear of hope.

Nothing slows pain's ropes pulling us toward our bodies:
we imagine springtime, mercy from the weather,
love beyond its own sake—
there is never enough of it, anyway—
only the scattershot of grief tessellating through
the earth, clattering as it jinks and slides.

II

The Dream

I dreamed he had wings:
big, white, full wings
that he kept tucked
small like a feathered backpack.

When he lay down
to me, I slowly caressed
each weary feather
with my fingers,
my soft lips, and hallowed
kiss. Each sinew, spent
from flying and sore,
received breath
I didn't know I had,
and then he was inside me,
and we flew
on arcs of whispers
that hold the night together.

When I awoke,
he was there
with deflated wings
like broken kite ribs
and torn, folded feathers.

As I stroked one
with my fingertip,
he turned to me,
and with a blink
of sleep-drenched eyes,
he disappeared.

HARBINGER

Suppose it were different.

Suppose it were my shape
you found as you looked out the window,

if night's soft gray
seeped into the day's cracks
as fall seems to creep up on leaves:
a gasp of red on green.

THE LONGEST DAY

Liquid hours unfurl like thin dough
over the prairie smitten with sun,
as if the horizon itself were only light.
Through the busy grass
quaking in the wind, birds coast, dive, peck, rise—
knowing the spaces
better than anything;
even the crimson poppies
never wishing for anything else
but to bloom, once.
Dirt below, light above,
only grass in the middle.
This is where the world ends or seems to.

We begin at the lip of memory;
ragged seams fray as we enter
and pull just one thin thread
before we're tangled. Nothing
to reckon with, this burl
of grass laced with wildflowers and faded green—
day's vast shroud draped over everything
we ever desired—
summer's shimmering gold.
I held light once,
up against the sky to see it hum.

Feet tether us to bodies,
to the earth,
hands to soil as it crumbles
through fisted fingers.
The longest day holds us
to two: the now and the coming—
one body, many forms.

Evanescence (with Clouds)

A day is nothing if not a disappearing act
held fast by ropes of sunlight and breeze until rain comes
or a tree coughs to shake night along;

then there are the shadows that feel like yesterday's distance
but become only apparitions when we haul them into light
or move beyond their pull—

I wish for mornings, still, days full of violets—
and the beautiful clouds, where in their always-
disappearing, their solemn ache, I find poems.

Long Dusks

I'm thinking about the moon
and its tradition of memory
while we rehearse for evening,
for summer's long dusks
when the grass hums in a green fermata
and the air is filled with marbles
of birdsong.

Now we're on the porch.
A piece of prairie grass hangs
lazily from your teeth.
Tonight the stars are heavy.
The sky bends under their weight.
We wait for rain, for tongues of wind
at the windows, stemming our wakefulness.

LOVE POEM WITH SUBJUNCTIVE

Today, it isn't easy to say I died

and then came back as the rectangle of light
spreading before dusk over your living room wall
or as the new spruce branches
I've grown to reach for you.

It's impossible to tell you

how last month I became a canary
alone, warbling above
the warm scent of your hair on the pillow
as night closed in.

If I become anything else,

it would be your breath on morning's mirror
watching the day peer over the horizon,
then crawl across the world.

Once, it was impossible to ask you

to wait for night to firm and fill,
to create space for the moon.

I could only close my eyes and wish,

think of the stars that once picked out our path
with their light.

A MATTER OF SEMANTICS

I want to rest in the hammocks between definitions,
between ghost and spirit, body and corpse.

A crow doesn't care that it's a crow and not a raven,
how black the slick of its feathers.
It knows how to crow in the sky across the wind,
how to gather discarded things and to keep or give.

They say getting rid of things can bring you joy,
that perhaps nothing is better than something.

But even the great nothing that orders it all
cannot make a heart (however imperfect) love
what it won't.

We can't blow breath into a ghost
and call it full of spirit.

The Weather Gods

It should be enough, the bits of breakfast,
the coffee cups tumbled into the sink,
the watermark on the couch pillow,
the wave from the window on the way to work.

It all should be enough, a matter of routine,
the things that come with it,
the things we do when doing is being
and being seems all there is to do.

It's kind of like the rain:
we love it for our gardens
or for evenings in deep July,
to sit together and hear its roar
on the roof and its drum on the earth
in the duvet of dark.

It can feel good, resolve—
until you find you're at the mercy of other forces,
the weather gods who summon rain
while you're changing a tire at the side of the road
in late November, cold and raw and sharp
or when it swells the rivers,
breaks the dams, swallows the earth.

MATING SEASON

Rumor has it that the female swans
have migrated to the river
to escape
the advances of their mates
who wait for them in the pond
out front.
(It's mating season.)

Despite the unfamiliar territory,
they glide peacefully
through the murky water;
one's neck is stained
beige from plunging all day.
It seems better
than having to keep herself
preened and groomed,
waiting for the insistent peacocking
of her lifelong mate to stop.

Do they remember
Zeus and Leda?
Do they carry the trauma
underneath their white feathers,
within the sinews of down?
Do their throats echo
her cries or the sounds
of her supplication, then fall silent,
defeated?

I wonder if I carry Leda's pain
within me, deep in my cells;
I wonder if the purpose of myth
is not to explain away,
displace,
but to find connection
across eons,
a thread to pull.

PROPHECIES BEFORE SPRING, IN RED AND WHITE

I've been saving some things for you.

A white feather from the day we saw the goose on the roof.
You said maybe things were coming true.

A single scarlet tulip
in a creamy white patch of late daffodils.

A cardinal's chirring in the air:
blood within us, blood around us—spring.

Spring's promise comes and goes and comes.
Winter kicks off its boots to run barefoot

through the new, sleepy grass and then
the trees, summer-thin and full of breath.

Zeus Contemplates His Encounter with Leda While Awaiting His Rape Trial

(Later, he would say)
she looked like a holiday,
bare in embrace;
girlish and slick,
she giggled until it was over.
Smudged smiles etched
into the skin,
carrying the scent
of bodies loved in full sun.

(Back in the clouds,
he remembered)
she hallowed his back
with her breath; she
unfolded each wing—
delicate as white brocade,
smooth as the sun
on the water—
with careful fingers
and pregnant pink lips
caressing each feather
each weary sinew
in holy consecration.

(After it was all over
and he flew back to his celestial palace,
he would remember)
that they slept, holy and restful
amidst a cathedral of blankets,
two halves of a broken whole.

SOMETHING LIKE LIGHT

Your hands move through prayer
like water in summer trees,
sparkling tessellations winking in the sky.

Today is the day I attend Mass
and say *Amen* without a heart.

The only church I've ever been to
is the one with the broken birds
and souls, with light as blue and calm as day,
lost love at first sight.

There is nothing holy
about a body beyond itself,
a body shorn clean of voice
and of light
as if by a lion's tongue.

You take my picture as I move
into the shadows,
so you can bury it
with the bones of your memory,
the dirt full of holes
to hide all the things we hope
our eyes reveal.

In springtime, the first thing I do
is scour the ground
for crocus fingers climbing sore
and weary out of the earth.

You ask me at the cusp of breathing
where will we go,

where will we go
when the night hides away

and the light is red as strawberries
in the slice of the summer sun,
quivering under the knife's cut,
a final rendering?

THE EYE

I looked for you in all the languages,
but you were not there.

I held a needle eye to eye
and through it searched the sky.

Only when I stopped looking did you appear,
quiet like a pearl in all this dark,

and then you disappeared
before I could tell you

everything I know about being alive:

my body an ocean, wide and deep, full of glints
and light and the roaming rhythm of comfort,

but it ends—
shoved up to the truest edge of the sky,
never crossing toward heaven, as if to say
no—there is no salvation.

I WORRIED ALL NIGHT ABOUT THE BIRDS

I worried all night about the birds:
they shivered on icy branches,
and I feared they would slip off
and tumble earthward, hitting
another branch as they fell.

I must have forgotten they could fly—
even in an accident of wind,
they could rely on their wings;
if they missed a branch,
they could always
fly to the next, right themselves
in the storm, or huddle in the nest,
hidden among branches.

It's funny the things we forget
or forget we remember—
especially when there's an ice storm
and you're next to me, asleep,
not gazing at the window
worrying about the birds.

That Day We Walked the Beach

Listen to the wind singing memory to sleep   its lullaby in the leaves
spring and summer are coming and so are you
rising from the fog and waiting for me
to find you just as I found you .   that day when we walked the beach
feet combing the sand   another wind to swirl my hair
your hand in the waves   Listen   to the gulls
heavy in the sky   their calls brief blessings
we walk long as the day stretching before us
light as far as the eyes hold
then dissolves into magic   Listen to it echo in the water   the air
our shapes on cragged rocks   peninsular in the sky
foam lacing the waves   Listen to the tide skirmish across the water
engraving the earth   down upon the sand again
we hold ourselves fast
against the coming of time   Listen
to hymns whispered in the horizon
as it hurls   hurtles across corduroy fields
careless as rocks   Listen for the tousle of pebbles
the sigh in summer
the song in clouds   I bury sinews of my memory in beads
chains I will wear as April peels into May
spring and summer are coming and so are you
the deep breath of spring the only sound I will hear   Listen
we are not what we believe   we are   we are roots come back
as light   as breath   as dust   as wind
longer than it all   Listen   prayer in the trees.

LATE SUMMER

Right below the pale horizon,
green floods the earth.
Wildflowers lace the roads,
and milkweed bulges with green chrysalides.

Maybe the only thing I'll ever believe is that
the wind loves the sea of grass—
the shape of its green memory
washed up on beaches as sea glass
or in trees' silhouettes in the hum
of summer heat, lazy in their sway,
framing the earth,
listening for lichen.

Maybe there's nothing beyond
but shapes on morning's light,
on branches that breathe into patterns
against the sky, then stillness.

PILLOW TALK (2)

He said
he wanted to keep me company
in my insomnia, so
we sat, knees mountains
in the bed,
hands held across
the valleys they made,
our bodies ink
on the pillows and creases.
I think it would be interesting
if you wrote a poem
about life before
women got their periods.

I said
nothing
because that has never
happened, and what
would life be like without it?
(This is what he says
when he thinks he is funny.)
But then I think of Venus
arising from a shell,
bobbing along the waves,
Adriatic green:
she had babies,
she had a womb
blood-red and holy
enough for twins.

He said
I worry about you
so much, awake at night
and he strokes my head,
his fingers tendrils
across my face.

I think
he writes me into existence
like the fashioning of angels,
(pale waxen skin
new against the silhouette
of morning)
a Venus without her period—
barren, virginal, fresh, and clean
as the night air
he breathes into his sleeping lungs.

Love Poem with Pansies

We are not only what we belong to.

We are bigger than that and yet so small,
like fingers of honeysuckle
tickling the vines that hug the house

and the fence and the birds
as the scent seeps out to dissolve
in the air. In lungs. In light.

Light conjures spiderwebs
when it wants us to notice it.

Notice it holy in the bend of trees.
Maybe the best thing about light is that it bends.
How could we ever stop without bending

along the curve of it all,
the curve of the earth at night?

Our eyes and ears and fingers
remind us and our tears how it all sounded
when we hid under curtains

of light. Of love. And there were wings
and pansies that kept velvet always as their bodies
fragrant as earth and day and new.

LOVE POEM FOR AN ALREADY-BROKEN HEART

This is how it starts: you become part of a distance,
like liquid air laid out in front of the vanishing point,
the echo of crows calling in an always-empty sky.

I'm not listening for them anymore. Instead, last night,
I took a glass of wine to bed, heard a brave robin outside
with summer in its voice. Somehow there is always a bird

in color, even as it hides in the shadows. We spill out
of the world like breeze seems always to fall out of trees.
If we go out far enough, we'll find each other.

THINGS THAT HAVE CHANGED THIS YEAR:
AN INCOMPLETE INVENTORY

Now, when I look at the pink palettes in sunsets,
I remember they're from chemicals in the atmosphere.

And then there's this grief—
the way it breathes only when I'm not looking,
grief for what's to come, what will always remain,
what will not be.

I didn't rake the leaves before it snowed,
and my backyard is now littered with dead leaves,
remnants of the garden, grackles and sparrows pecking at the dirt.

But I have learned to notice morning turning water to light
over the lake on my way to work,

so I believe in ghosts, though only the kind
that haunt hearts, make them heavy.

Walking without You for the First Time

My shadow props me up in all this light—
light that used to taste like butter in our mouths
or that often hid behind us in a game of chase.
Once we ran after a dog we thought was lost,
traipsing through soggy grass for nearly half a mile,
yelling and calling in the wind, only to find
the owner hidden just around the corner,
letting the dog run.
We laughed, kept going.

We always kept going,
as if the world were a machine
powered by the crooked leans of our bodies
and the stamp of our feet along the path,
drowned blue hem of sky racing along with us,
bees and birds thrilling to open air,
wind like a huge white sail with open arms and full, full.

It's all still whirring along. The ocean's still at it,
folding and unfolding. Dogs still bark, catch frisbees
in their mouths. In the early parts of dusk,
tucked in the golden glow of their evening houses,
people still eat dinner, scrape plates into sinks.

The wind still shudders through trees, leaves
flirt this way and that, until it's time to loosen
and fall, doing so gracefully.

TITLE INDEX

First Line Index

W

Y

CPSIA information can be obtained
at www.ICGtesting.com
Printed in the USA
BVHW071048270123
657287BV00017B/708

9 781594 980930